# Beyond the Galleons

ᜐ᜔ᜆᜓᜎᜓᜌᜓᜊᜓᜆᜓ᜔ᜈᜄᜒᜎᜒᜌᜓ

*by*

## Isabel Cristina Legarda

YELLOW ARROW

>>———▶

PUBLISHING

Baltimore, Maryland, USA

*For my family,*
*there and here*

# Contents

# Acknowledgments

*Diaspora Baby Blues* (online), March 2021
"Pantoum for a Childhood Elsewhere"

*The Ignatian*, March 2021
"Reading Tutorial for a Jesuit Missionary, 1668"

*Moida* (online), August 2021
"Kain Na"

*Riksha* (online), August 2021
"Writing the Icon of Lakapati"

*Aletheia Literary Quarterly* (online), October 2021
"Unmoored"

*HeartWood Literary* (online), November 2021
"Far from the Tree"

*Smartish Pace*, February 2022
"Boondocks"
(finalist for the Beullah Rose Poetry Prize)

*Equinox* (online), March 2022
"Angel Island, San Francisco Bay"

*Matter Monthly* (online), July 2022
"Pacification, 1901," "Louisiana Purchase Exposition,
St. Louis, 1904," and "Bud Dajo, 1906"

*Superpresent*, December 2022
"What We Swallowed" and "Bagoong Alamang"

*Clepsydra* (online), January 2023
"Before the Galleon Run"

Gasher Press, *Cherry Moon Anthology,* May 2023
"Song of the Last Boatbuilder"

*West Trestle Review* (online), November 2023
"Saint Malo, Louisiana"

*Voices de la Luna* (print and online), March 2024
"Manila North"

I would like to thank the extraordinary readers and editors at Yellow Arrow Publishing, especially Kapua Iao, Jill Earl, Angela Firman, Marylou Fusco, Annie Marhefka, Melissa Nuñez, Ann Quinn, Kait Quinn, and Mel Silberger, whose precision, insight, and encouragement helped create—and helped me truly love—this book. I am deeply grateful to creative director Alexa Laharty for capturing the soul of this collection with her beautiful cover design.

I owe special thanks to poet and mentor Caroline Goodwin and to fellow writers from her poetry workshop—Diana Feiger, Alison Hurwitz, Kathleen McGraw, Peg Padnos, and Elisabeth Preston-Hsu—who helped bring so many of these poems into the world.

I also owe profound gratitude to my husband, Eric Thompson, for his faith, feedback, and love.

# BEYOND THE GALLEONS

<u>Part I</u>

ᜀᜅ᜔ ᜑᜒᜈ᜔ᜇᜒ ᜋᜇᜓᜈᜓᜅ᜔ ᜎᜓᜋᜒᜅᜓᜈ᜔ ᜐ ᜉᜒᜈᜅ᜔ᜄᜎᜒᜅᜈ᜔
ᜑᜒᜈ᜔ᜇᜒ ᜋᜃᜇᜇᜆᜒᜅ᜔ ᜐ ᜉᜇᜓᜇᜓᜂᜈᜈ᜔

Ang hindi marunong lumingon sa pinanggalingan
hindi makararating sa paroroonan.

Those who don't know how to look back at their
origins will be unable to reach their destination.

# Pantoum for a Childhood Elsewhere

All it takes is one sip to bring it all back—
the reedy smell of newly cut grass,
a rooster crowing in the neighbor's yard,
a hot, sweet ensaymada topped with sugar and melted cheese—

the reedy smell of newly cut grass
in the shade of a fallen mango tree,
a hot, sweet ensaymada topped with sugar and melted cheese,
a cup of chocolate stirred with a batidor.

In the shade of a fallen mango tree,
there is bliss to be found
in a cup of chocolate stirred with a batidor
for hours, a labor of drop-by-drop patience.

There is bliss to be found
in a quiet morning of writing
for hours, a labor of drop-by-drop patience,
with a view of palm trees and purple hills.

In a quiet morning of writing
we can go home again, to a past that still lives,
with a view of palm trees and purple hills,
away from the cold, away from being foreign.

We can go home again to a past that still lives,
to a rooster crowing in a neighbor's yard,
away from the cold, away from being foreign.
All it takes is one sip to bring it all back.

# Cartography

On my grandmother's island
people once believed in soul families:

our spirits, they said, come to this earth
connected, like bodies linked by bloodlines,

our ley lines to one another,
chart of an undiscovered world.

We spend our lives searching, clinging,
grieving, longing for our soulmates'

touch on our skin;
we wander the world electric

secretly mapping our love
in the hope of meeting again.

# Reading Tutorial for a Jesuit Missionary, 1668

This is what you wrote, Father Alcina,
about learning how to read our script:
Su leer es adivinar más que pronunciar –
reading it is a guessing game, you complained.

It's not that the characters are hard to remember –
with only seventeen, even you admitted
es fácil de aprender; but with an alphasyllabary,
the vowels are hidden from view.

Es muy dificil el leer porque, como hemos dicho, lo más es suplir:
"very difficult to read," you wrote, because the reader
must supply what's hidden, discern meanings
by intimately knowing them already.

ᜑᜒᜇᜒᜈᜋᜋᜑᜒᜇᜃᜓᜐᜈᜃᜐ ᜑᜒᜇᜒᜈᜃᜒᜃᜒᜆ

Hindi naman mahirap kung sanay ka sa hindi nakikita.
It's not so hard when you are accustomed to the unseen.
You worship it from afar; we live with it day to day.

Tabi tabi po, we say, to make sure we don't step
on a spirit in our path. Tao po, we announce, to assure
we are of this world and will not harm.
Puwera usog, we pronounce over our crying infants,
in tacit acknowledgment that unseen forces are real.

You fear magic and ghosts; to us, those are just words
for reality and life. You noted with surprise,
Algunos, y más las mujeres, leen con destreza y sin tropezar:
the women, especially, read without stumbling.

But of course. We are experts at discerning the unseen.
We are the vowels of our villages' lives,
supplying meaning and depth, sometimes invisibly,
but ever-present in the stories unfolding.

Our people, Father Alcina, are the syllables
you are failing to read, the meanings
you don't know well enough to guess.
To divine us, you must be willing to know
and love the glory you cannot see.
Only then. Only then will you understand.

ꦮꦤꦴꦩꦴꦤꦴꦥꦴꦱꦴꦤꦴꦤꦴꦮꦴꦮꦴꦤꦴꦮꦴ

# Writing the Icon of Lakapati

The Spaniards arrived and encountered fecundity –
the lush greenness of taro terraces,
ripe fruits falling from branches surrendering
to the weight of their abundance, trees
with green leaves so large
we could shelter beneath them in the rain,
an uninhibited earth almost flamboyant
in its yielding and giving,
endless green over lowlands and mountains,
and a bluish-green at the shore.

You were the green goddess who raised their suspicion,
defied comprehension, challenged belief,
a man who was a woman,
a woman with the power to feed the green world,
to heal, deal with evil, see the future, rise above the past
like the shaman women of all sexes who recited your truths,
for whom intimacy and creativity and poetry were no threat.

The priests from Spain worshipped an ivory man
nailed to wood, a pallor and confinement so foreign
to a people whose faith was in motion, celebration, and life.
The priests could not comprehend our joy, our equality,
the power of our women. When we continued to hold up
our children to you, praying
Lakapati pakanin mo, huwag mong gutumin—
Lakapati feed them, let them not hunger—
they told us your new name was Espíritu Santo,
moved you out of reach
from rows of green unhusked rice.

We have almost forgotten you.
We prepare wood for an icon of you –
not the dead wood of the cross
but the living wood of the jungles,
our shelter and warmth;
the linen over it not a death shroud
but a mantle of protection;
layers of gesso, gold leaf, and green
egg tempera to complete our blasphemous
glorification of you, transgender goddess
of fertile lands and hearts,
kind spirit of our people,
woman of our dreams.

# Before the Galleon Run

In the shipyards of Cebu, Cavite, and Sorsogon,
the hardwood of felled cashew trees
holds the promise of perilous voyages.

When all this began, our craftsmen,
accustomed to the karakoa's double outriggers
and the crab-claw sails of balangays,
had never built such massive ships,
with names like El Poderoso,
La Princesa, San Carlos Borromeo.

Even vessels that have made the crossing
many times, appearing long awaited
over far horizons, sails triumphant
on giant masts, have been dashed to pieces
on the rocks east of Luzon or near Santa Catalina,

their silver and silks, beeswax and porcelain,
their eight-year-old page boys, teenage apprentices,
and Filipino sailors in their prime (for Spaniards here
are tough to recruit for their own ventures)
forgotten under the rolling swells.

How do they board these galleons
knowing rough oceans lie ahead?

For whom will they cry alone in the water,
pelted with lashing rain, no land to rest on,
swallowed whole by the deep, black sea?

The cold. The unbearable cold.
How heartless, how monstrous, the merciless sea.
Have mercy, maawa ka, merciless sea.

# What We Swallowed

We said pabada instead of fabada
and parol instead of farol,
and though they had trouble
with the n-g in nga and halang
and nangangailangan, somehow
only our difficulties with their fricatives
signified inferiority.

At table we laid out slices of sour mango
and bowls of bagoong—a beloved combination
best shared among friends—but they
couldn't stomach the condiment's smell.

Yet they watched in fascination
as we took a squid apart,
removing the crystalline quill
from its core and preserving the ink sac
for our sauce. (A Jesuit brought notes of this
back to Iberia, where the gift of calamares
en su tinta subsequently graced
the kitchens of Spain.)

Like their manor lords who took
the choicest cuts of meat, they left us
with intestines, liver, lungs, and heart.
From them we learned to make
bofe de res – bopis, we called it.
We took hot morsels of heart
on our tongues, amen, amen,
our tongues that could not speak
like theirs, tasting hearts like warriors,
our tongues silenced inside our mouths,
our hearts wailing silently
in our mother tongue.

# Letter Fragments, Fr. Alcina to the Jesuit Superior General, July 1, 1674

I believe I am not long for this world.
I have learned, Father Oliva, much about faith.

Belief in the absurd is easy.
Even Tertullian wrote of Christ's rising
certum est quia impossibile.

But to teach, to write, to hope
that we have done good with our lives,
when our words and acts leave us
and enter a void – these take more faith.

Real Presence is easier.

More than forty years
I have lived with my beloved Visayans,
listening to their secret tears,
their sins, their fears, christening infants
that would bring a smile to even the gruffest
among us, burying their dead. Even in sorrow
they are full of joy.

There were days when hardheadedness
or petty complaints would make me want
to bang my head on the bell tower.
Nevertheless, they are glorious,
and I love them all.

How can I know if it is enough?
I suppose, Father Oliva, we can never know.
The night is falling. The day is almost over.
I pray for the Lord's blessing upon you.

Ad majorem Dei gloriam
– Francisco Ignacio Alcina

# The Wreck of the Santo Cristo de Burgos

A galleon named
for a miraculous statue
found at sea
shattered off the coast
of Oregon.

Shards of porcelain
wash up on the sand
from time to time –
a trail of crumbs
from a lost tea ceremony,

bone fragments
of forgotten sailors
wandering among
waterlogged timbers below,
still trying to hoist their sails.

# Saint Malo, Louisiana

*a burning haibun**

Salt waters have always been our home, our blood. In the time of myths and heroes' songs, whale sharks and manta rays guided our boats. For generations now, we've manned the giant galleons, but we are weary; our blistered fingers bleed. We turn to our mother sea to save us, to wash off the salt of our sweat. We jump into her arms, escape to the briny marshlands. Here we'll build our bahay kubo on stilts and live free. The mosquitos and storms will remind us of home, and the plentiful shrimp.

The people here don't know the Shrimp Dance. We boil the shrimp, dry them for days in the sun, then grind the shells off underfoot. Les enseñaremos. The pink flesh will help them forget our brown skin.

A hundred years from now, we'll still be far from our native shores, we oarsmen, whalers, explorers like our ancestors, pearling for our women, pining for our home. Manilamen, they'll call us, as they chase their white whales. We'll work on the oceans until we die. In a thousand years, perhaps, we'll still be guided by stars; our ships will soar through nebulae like galleons gliding through smooth seas. We'll keep our sails unfurled until the end of time.

---

* The burning haibun is a form originated by poet torrin a. greathouse.

Salt waters have always been 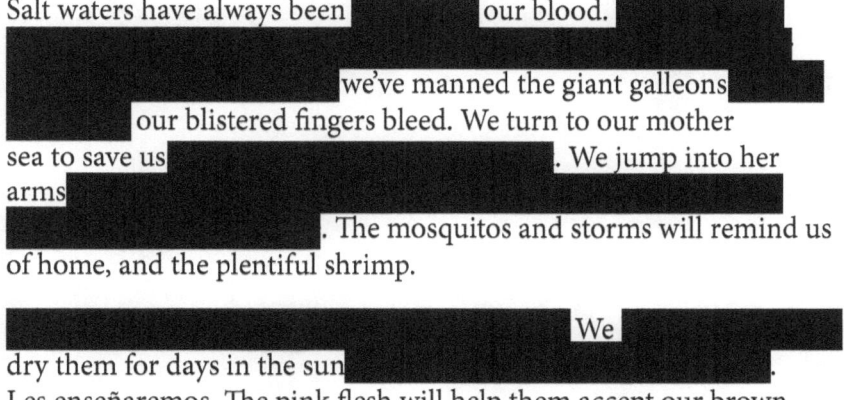 our blood.

we've manned the giant galleons
our blistered fingers bleed. We turn to our mother
sea to save us. We jump into her
arms
. The mosquitos and storms will remind us
of home, and the plentiful shrimp.

We
dry them for days in the sun.
Les enseñaremos. The pink flesh will help them accept our brown
skin.

A hundred years from now, we'll still be far from our native shores,

pining for our home.
We'll work on the oceans until we die.
our ships will
soar through nebulae. We'll
keep our sails unfurled.


mother sea save us
help them respect our brown skin
keep our sails unfurled

# Part II

ᜃ᜔ᜐᜋ ᜈᜋᜒᜈ᜔ ᜀᜇᜏ᜔ᜀᜇᜏ᜔ ᜀᜅ᜔ ᜑᜒᜈ᜔ᜇᜒ ᜈᜃᜒᜃᜒᜆ

Kasama namin araw-araw ang hindi nakikita.

We live with the unseen day to day.

# Boondocks

## I.

We hear the word and think
uncouth, naive, unsophisticated,

ramshackle huts off the grid,
prints of bare feet pressed
to dirt roads, scattered
corn husks, the smell
of burning wood, skin
prickling against the elements –

where a bad fall can mean
the end of life.

## II.

Bundok means "mountain" in Tagalog.
Mountains meant hiding places
for Filipinos fighting for home.

American soldiers had words for them.
Guerrillas. Insurrectos. Ladrones.
Uncouth. Unsophisticated. Uncivilized.

In American minds and mouths
the mountain, too, transmogrified
into contemptible, suspicious.

III.
When bundok became the boondocks

lost was the mountain as holy ground
in the civilized world
of "water cures" and massacres;

denied, the wisdoms of the wilderness –
tree root, tattered wing, water flow
on rock and silt, the thrum
of creatures stumbling across
the world in tiny steps, the rippling
of diaphanous fins, ever homing;

forgotten, like a desolate plot of earth,
the worth of a person pining for home.

# Pacification, 1901

On Immaculate Conception Day
just in time to ruin Christmas
came the order to move
to "zones of protection"
– a disingenuous phrase.

You asked us to fetch petrol, then
doused our homes and burned them down.
Our paper faroles, already hanging,
quickly flared amid the flames.
Our desecrated memories
the color of ash.

Near the concentration camp
a blister on my heel burst open
and for a moment the pain was gone.
A minute later, excruciating hurt
even worse than before, as with each step
my shoe rubbed raw the broken surface.

The crowding was an abomination –
30,000 where only 3,000 should have been.
We were packed together so close
in our living spaces that I could count
the goose bumps on my neighbor's skin
when he took ill with fever and chills,
his pallet drenched
with a sick-smelling sweat.

Within six months the parish burial records
in Batangas and Lipa more than doubled
from the camps, where cholera and measles
festered. Everyone had diarrhea, and if
we weren't vomiting from disease
we were throwing up from the stench
and filth in which we lived.

How I longed for clean water
to wash with and drink.
I would have asked for a jug
if I could have been sure
you wouldn't, out of habit,
hold me down at each extremity
to force the water down my throat.

# Louisiana Purchase Exposition, St. Louis, 1904

You made us eat dog
so moms with giant feathers in their hats
could point to us and exclaim
to their astonished kids,
"Look at how these savages live!"
At the edge of our enclosure, families
glanced at guidebooks you wrote
and whispered, wide-eyed,
*Head hunters!* – their mouths
agape with fascination.

Our forty-seven acre reservation
brought in more revenue than anything
else at the fair, even with all
the hot dogs and ice cream cones,
forty brands of ketchup on display,
Ferris wheel, carousel, dirigible,
dinosaur bones, trains, and a funhouse
where fairgoers could visit "Hell."
There was noise everywhere
from marching bands, barkers,
throngs of people. I missed
the highlands of Bontoc,
the mists and green slopes,
the quiet, and the scent of pine.

Two of us died on the way here,
frozen in the boxcar you failed to heat.
Some got beriberi, smallpox, pneumonia.
No one at the fairground asked if we were cold.
They complained we were half naked.
You people were so ill at ease
with your own bodies, so unlike us,

so afraid of your humanity.

You made us dance in our loincloths
several times a day and compete
in unfamiliar games we couldn't help but lose.
Outwardly we smiled at you, but inside:
a swirling pool of shame, the surface
rippling with each stare, the depths
a dark and secret muck
embedding our despair.

You measured our skulls
to prove we were stupider.
I only learned later
you conspired to collect them
and take our brains after we died.
You knew, you anticipated,
that some of us would die,
and you felt entitled to dispose
of us as you wanted, without asking—
a femur here, a calvarium there.
Our bodies didn't matter. You treated us
like dogs, consuming us, so even in death
I was still in a zoo, exposed,
my flesh boiled off and thrown away,
my skull indistinguishable on a shelf
with a thousand others, still subject
to scrutiny and gawking and judgment.

I want the last word.
I want my skull back.

# Bud Dajo, 1906

I said to my son on our ascent,
the volcano is extinct –
we need no longer fear it.
Immediately he felt at ease.
He had faith in his mother's word.
He trusted me to keep him safe.
We walked in the path of Allah,
and for that moment, the path
was an uphill climb.
We scaled the heart-crushing slope,
sometimes crawling on our bellies
to press against the steep angle.
I paused many times
to catch my breath.

In the crater our crops thrived –
potatoes and rice nourished by spring water.
We greeted each green growing thing
with the same joy we shared
with newcomers from Jolo.
We were only a few hundred
in the beginning, but by the end
we were a thousand,
our very own barangay
in the bowl of a dead volcano,
turning ourselves five times a day
toward the sunset ridge to say our prayers.

All of us, women and men alike,
were ready to fight and die for our faith.
We had seashell grenades filled
with black powder, knives and spears,
short swords, a few rifles. But our tiny cannons,

almost like toys on the crater's edge,
were no match for the shelling that began.
The booming and shaking scared us as much
as a lava explosion, and our children began
to cry. I wished I could hold my six-year-old
in my lap, feel his heart like a hummingbird
against my chest, and tell him everything
would be all right.

But how could it have been,
when we were inside a crater,
and you fired at us from the rim.
You who had called us,
when your grand project started,
your little brown brothers. We all know
what happens to your little brown brothers.
Look at Wounded Knee. Look at Samar,
where your General Smith said
*the more you kill and burn*
*the better it will please me.*
We had already heard from the north
of your occupation, concentration camps,
water torture, genocide, the order
to *kill everyone over ten.*
Predictably, that day in Bud Dajo,
when we were screaming inside
the crater and you were a battalion
of bayonets through and through us,
only six of us survived.

In a photograph of you
standing over our corpses
—a woman's exposed breast,
perhaps mine, in the center—
your faces are hard to read.

The image is too grainy and old
to show the stark contrast
between a troop of white men,
hands on hips, and a ditch of brown
Muslims, five layers of bodies deep,
your little brown brothers and sisters
in a crater we had made our home,
shot for refusing to submit to you.

My son was only six. I can't
find him in the picture.

# Angel Island, San Francisco Bay

The abandoned buildings are haunted,
crumbling steadily, their lifelessness
eerie and wrong, the bloodred hospital
now a dilapidated house – empty rooms,
rubble, cracked wood, plaster falling off
to reveal the broken bones of the place.
Even the serpentine quarry holds
only the ghosts of ghosts.

The immigration station,
"Guardian of the Western Gate,"
was where reasons could be rooted out—
trachoma, filariasis, being Chinese—
to turn undesirables away.
People were sometimes stranded here
for years, belonging nowhere,
trapped in a concentration camp
with many of the usual indignities:
separation of family members; terrible
food; rows of bunks like storage shelves;
medical exams of pubic areas to prove
age in Asians, the forever young;
nauseous elixirs against hookworm;
hunger; madness; experimentation
without consent.

No wonder the Chinese bride of legend,
denied entry to the mainland, hanged
herself in the women's bathroom
and wails there still. Listen closely
to hear her banging on the pipes.
The prisoners' voices are etched
into the barracks' wooden walls,

Chinese characters carved deeply in,
testament that even here, even then,
sorrow bled out as poetry.

# Far from the Tree

*for my mother*

Orange clouds: not sunset,
but Manila burning in the distance.

You and your mother fled to Taal
through coconut groves that night.

From the bottom of a ravine
you heard the people screaming,

flushed from sugarcane fields
on fire, shot as they ran out.

How did you get through that night?
How can I be brave like you

when just entering a room
full of people frightens me?

They might as well be coconut palms
looming in the dark.

*Nada* you'll say to me, your shorthand
for *You've got this.* Easy for you to say.

You played ball with your father's ghost
when you were only three.

# Memorare

*Remember, O Most Gracious Virgin Mary*

they raped us fifteen times a day.
"Comfort women" – who chose
such a cruel moniker?

*never was it known that anyone*

who sobbed or screamed
or stared into space, corpse-like
during the violence

*who fled to your protection*
*implored your help*

spat on, pissed on,
split by bayonets
urethra to sternum

*was left unaided.*

But us – what of us?

*O Mother of the Word Incarnate*

where were you when we
were being crucified
and we wept your rosaries
ceaselessly?

*Hail Mary, full of grace*
*the Lord is with you*

But not with us. Why not with us?

*Turn, then, most gracious Advocate,*
*thine eyes of mercy toward us*

Pray for us
sufferers, sex slaves, survivors

*now and until the hour of our death*
*now and until the hour of our death*

# Manila American Cemetery, Fort Bonifacio

It's complicated,
this business of colonial rule.

We can grit our teeth
at every instance they called us
*little brown brothers,*
bristle at the sneers and condescension,
the expectation of our incompetence,
deplore *kill everyone over ten,*
and the way Virchow asked Rizal,
*May I measure your skull;*
rail against every letter to the States
containing a casual n-word.

But here are 17,206 graves.

At the very least, here, our words
must fail us.

# Part III

ᜃᜋᜒ ᜀᜌ᜔ ᜀᜅ᜔ ᜋ᜔ᜄ ᜉᜆᜒᜈᜒᜄ᜔ ᜈ ᜎᜄᜒᜅ᜔ ᜈᜇᜓᜍᜓᜂᜈ᜔
ᜐ ᜋ᜔ᜄ ᜃᜓᜏᜒᜈ᜔ᜆᜓᜅ᜔ ᜈᜄ᜔ᜎᜎᜑᜇ᜔

Kami ay ang mga patinig na laging naroroon
sa mga kuwentong naglalahad.

We are the vowels ever-present
in stories unfolding.

# How to Fit In in America

*instructions for a young hopeful*

1. Come over. Leave behind the bibingka,
the green mangoes and salty, smelly bagoong,
the savory empanadas from Bulacan
made with that dough they call kaliskis
for its flakiness, like scales, or shards,
or squama. Don't let the smell of patis
get on your clothes. And whatever you do,
don't let your new friends see
the sliced hot dogs and sugar
in your spaghetti sauce.

2. Get rid of your accent. Say wodder,
not wa-ter, despite the fact that the "t"
is there in black and white.
Don't let them hear you talk
the way you talk at home.
Then learn to grit your teeth when later
someone says, "but you have no accent."

3. When the headmistress nun
at your Catholic school, who wears
an elegant dress instead of a habit
and coiffes her hair like Callas,
is doing a verbal screening test of sorts
by reading you a list of words,
and she instructs you to tell her
when you hear a word you don't know,
be honest. Listen. And wait. And wait.
Because you'll know all the words.
Then she'll think you're stupid
(or deaf) and say, trying to be polite,

"I just wanted to be sure you understood
the directions." Tell her you understood,
but you hadn't yet heard
a word you didn't know.

4. Behave. Never pray the rosary
where people can see you.
Try not to start decorating for Christmas
in September. When you're over
at other people's houses, don't act
like an unofficial commentator
and reiterate what's happening
on the TV shows everyone's watching.
Leave that to Lola at home, where the two of you
can laugh together in peace.
Do keep greeting people's parents
when you arrive and when you leave.
Some things you are just going to have to hang on to.

5. Laugh at everyone's jokes.
But try not to laugh at *everything*,
the way you're used to,
because then they'll get suspicious
and won't understand.
Be a fan of *Star Wars* and sitcoms
and talk about the the game, or
celebrity scandals, or the latest deal
at Dunkin' Donuts. In English.
With no accent.

Finally:

6. Topically whiten your skin and surgically
change the shape of your eyes.
Then you can forget about one through five.
You'll be acceptable.
You'll blend right in.
That's what you want,
isn't it?

# Manila North

In the north cemetery
a makeshift village –
sari-sari stores in abandoned crypts,
gawkers eating chocolate-covered ice cream bars
as someone is laid to rest,
children playing in the street.

One of the old-timers has a key
to a pyramidal mausoleum
at the far end of a tree-lined avenue.
The entire family tree is here –
ancestors only known by name,
their bodies in fragments,
their hurts forgotten.

Outside the sunlight is bright
over cemetery villagers
sweeping leaves. Untold stories
haunt the air, moving through the crypts
like breath, whispering, their secrets
rippling through the living
and the dead.

# All Souls

Picnic at a cemetery south of Manila
with steamed pork buns, uncut
noodles (for long life), rice flour sweets,

Royal Tru-Orange, and Fress Gusto
root beer. We sit on a colorful banig
in the shade of a yellowing canopy.

The grass, too, uncut.

In front of my great-grandparents'
graves, the kids splash around
with the groundskeeper's hose.

I only know the story in fragments.
She was a saint, they said, my Chinese-Filipina
great-grandmother with a Spanish first name:

Bernabela.

Long after she was gone, lost
to her heart's spasms
one New Year's Eve,

her husband, tall and terrifying,
with a nose like an eagle's beak,
would house-sit for us sometimes.

I never heard him say a word.

All I knew of their marriage
was that one time, when she was sick,
he put his hand on hers, and

she snatched it away like one burned.
She had once told my mother
jealousy should remain concealed –

ang selos ay hindi pinapakita.

With her sister in a sepia picture,
she smiles as if unhurt, the secret jealousy
simmering between them.

Her sister frowns at the camera, defiant.
Great-grandmother was always
the sweeter of the two.

They'd go arm in arm to Mass every day.

For years none of us put the pieces
together – their two children raised as twins,
born the same day.

In another sepia photo, the babies in their arms:
great-grandmother smiling, her sister scowling,
hovering, always near, never near enough.

Each "twin" thought she was great-grandmother's favorite.

We eat and drink in the canopy's shade
and contemplate the three sarcophagi,
great-grandfather between his wife

and her sister, three lovers long dead,
their agonies, too, asleep at last, the desires
among them that seemed so vast

not even a speck of dust.

# Unmoored

No ancient maps said *Here be dragons*, save one:
the sixteenth-century globe in the library on Fifth.
To venture toward lurking beasts in deeps and jungles
far away took arrogance, bravery, and ballast.
Sitting on a wall along the shore at Rockport,
I count the ballast stones below, piled centuries ago
beneath the surface, discarded from wooden ships
in exchange for the glamor of gold. I spy one
whose addition might have made the difference
between a journey completed and a journey lost,
its heft and gravity sorely needed to steady a vessel
that, otherwise, would be tossed off course
by menacing swells. Rock overboard, keel tilts
just enough, a world wobbling on its axis.
I lose my footing. Cartography won't help.
*Hic sunt dracones*, the map still says, the one
that only I can see. Fantastic creatures with twisted bodies
and garish colors adorn the margins of my thoughts,
but I am adrift in my own uncharted waves,
my sails sagging and my ballast lost.
I want so badly to say *Don't go*. I distract myself
with pointless mathematics: fifteen drops in a milliliter,
seventy-five in a teaspoon, an ocean of billions below
to traverse, countless as the stars sparkling above.
I navigate by them, as the ancients did, and disregard
the blackened sea. Alone on the water with lifeboat
and oar, salt on my face, hoping for safe harbor,
I brush the water and salt away and paddle
toward dragons without you.

# Street Food in Quiapo

Sidewalk vendors urge throngs of passersby
Bili na! Bili na! Bili na!
Shoppers have to turn sideways
just to get past each other.

                    Under giant multicolored umbrellas,
                         piles of red chilis, purple onions,
                                        green calamansi,
hanging T-shirts, flip-flops,
baskets, brooms in bunches,
capiz shell lanterns, parakeets in a cage.

A riot of smells from food at every turn:
dried squid on a skewer, charred on a grill
then doused with vinegar-soaked onions and chilis;

                    duck eggs, plain or fertilized,
                    containing feathery embryos,
                    the broth just inside the shell
                         a concentrated soup;
glass noodles, brown noodles,
noodles bright orange with atchuete;
kwek-kwek, sisig, rice cakes, barbecue,
a giant vat of fish balls rolling in hot oil;

                    smoke from the stalls and the plaza,
               noise from voices, vehicles honking, sizzling
          flesh, and the Quiapo Church loudspeaker,
               loud enough to drown out all thought.

               The
     gleaming white church, solid and silent
in the square, stands          unperturbed by the din.

People clamor for food and clothing, yes;
but in the maze of market stalls
crowding the church's hem,
pilgrims milling about also long for love and luck,
magic solutions, a reason, a way to believe.

In the shadow of the Black Nazarene,
colors and cacophony in perpetual motion: vendors' tables
crammed with love amulets, fertility charms, statues
of the baby Jesus, bracelets infused with good fortune,
bundles of candles in every color,

prayers sold
where spells won't do.

When miracles and magic prove elusive
women in the back of Quiapo church
offer to storm the heavens for a few coins.

Their lips are never still.
A few pesos for your deepest secrets,
your heart's most urgent desire.

The cooking goes on all day.
Garbage burns. Incense ascends
from swinging censers.

Smoke rising, always,
from the altar, the pews,
the streets, the stalls.

Heart in ardent supplication
beneath every smiling face.

Prayers.

Prayers bubbling
below the surface

bursting into the smoky air

                                        ascending
                                    disappearing
                        while the hungry burn below.

# Bagoong Alamang

Nothing floods a pinoy mouth more quickly
—not the most succulent meats or sweets—
than the mere thought of this stinky, salty
concoction, reddish-brown or purplish-pink
with angkak.

He could not countenance the smell –
like a fishy corpse, he thought, pungent,
putrefying. The tapayan—large-mouthed
earthenware jars with tight lids
they use to ferment the krill—
can indeed be used to bury the dead,
but I reminded him fermentation is not decay.

In the waters off Pangasinan or far to the north,
where the Cagayan River empties into the sea,
fishermen drag their starboard nets to capture
the tiny shrimp to be washed and dried and ground
and salted, then sealed in jars for weeks. Black jellyfish
caught alongside them are thrown back into the sea.
Later, the patis skimmed off, the muck is sautéed
with garlic, vinegar, chilis, and cane sugar
to make bagoong alamang. It smells – how it smells!
But oh, the taste. . . .
                    Once he tried it, he understood.
No mere condiment, bagoong becomes a meal's soul
in the way mere salt cannot, the secret of a dish's complexity,
an ocean spirit possessing the food. It casts a spell,
a brine of desire—as happens, perhaps, with oysters
or caviar—all of these but shadows of the true delight;
swell of ocean rising, sea minerals on his tongue,
his breath on my thighs the wind on a shore
wet with foam, waves rolling, returning, his body
covering mine, the salt, the sweetness,
the rising tide, my body vanishing at last,
spray over surf.

# Kain Na

A coworker from my country of birth
greets me in the corridor
with a raise of the eyebrows and
"Kumain ka na?"

Not hello, not how are you,
but "Have you eaten already?"
We smile at each other
though the answer is *no*,
delighting in this not-so-secret code

that holds thousands of years
of communal concern,
prayers to a transgender goddess
for rice in abundance
to feed hungry children,

centuries of going to morning Mass,
then bibingka and salabat,
a rice cake and ginger tea afterward,
the salted egg on top a counterpoint
to the buttery sweetness of every bite
and the tang of each warm and comforting sip,

decades of sharing four meals a day:
almusal, tanghalian, meryenda, hapunan.
Food, food everywhere, food when we're born,
food when we die, in the very funeral chapels
in which our bodies lie, food
to pay a visit or to welcome a guest,
pancit, lumpia, adobo, kaldereta,
bagoong, hopia, siopao, sapin-sapin.

We are obsessed with food
because it holds us together,
a knowing smack on the shoulder
with a generous helping of mirth,
or the comfort of not being alone
with our tears; food is joy, food is love,
fussy mothers and yayas and titas and lolas
who all care, perhaps too much;
who all mean to say, *you are loved.*

One time on the Amtrak train to New York
the snack bar attendant offered me his suman,
sweet sticky rice wrapped in banana leaf,
simply because we spoke the same mother tongue.

That recognition of a word,
an expression, a sound,
is so precious, especially
far away from home –
at first, a burst of surprise,
like the first citrusy bite of kinilaw,
then deep comfort and relief
like home-cooked arroz caldo,
warm and tasty in our mouths.

So when we in our diaspora
see one another, of course we ask,
"Kumain ka na?"
For if the answer is yes,
we can be happy and at ease,
and if no, we can at least offer
sympathy, or hope—

all of which
is love, love cut open,
love spread thickly
like ube jam, love
stirred and folded
and spooned out to the world,
consumed and consuming,
sliced to pieces yet still whole,
an egg cracked open,
the fragrance of a pandan leaf,
a bowl of rice,
a grain.

# Song of the Last Boatbuilder

If our creations are forbidden,
our children will forget.

They will forget how the dowel at one point of contact
matters along the plank's entire length;

how to sypher the edges of wood just so,
such that each strip fits fast and tight against another;

how high to make the bulwarks,
how wide all the apertures;

how turning to starboard means
a push against port;

how our sails need strong but gentle hands
to find the ocean wind.

Who will teach them to hold up their palms
to the sky and peer at our ancestors' souls?

When we are gone,
who will place our hulls in the water?

How will they know where to go?

# Feast of San Lorenzo Ruiz,
# Binondo Church, September 28, 2021

The miracle child showed up
to Mass – Cecilia Alegria
Policarpio, now fortysomething,
but at age two,
limp and listless
from water in the brain,
cured after prayers
to the parish's
martyred scribe.

One miracle
instead of the usual two
would suffice for sainthood,
Lorenzo's intercession
for a girl's congested brain
befitting, considering
his manner of death:

ana-tsurushi, hung
upside down, body
bound
all along its length,
head and shoulders
in a pit,

cut off from the world,

one hand left free
to signal surrender.

The escribano of Binondo
would not recant –

> Kahit isang libo mang buhay mayroon ako
> ay iaalay ko pa rin sa Kanya.

Missionaries sent word
of his words
back to Manila:
si mille vitas haberem
cunctas ei offerrem.

Over hours, then days,
an incision in his head
forestalling congestion
just enough,
his brain began to write,
at first only able
to copy out psalms –

> *But I am a worm and not a man . . .*

> *Strong bulls of Bashan encircle me . . .*

> *I am poured out like water*
> *and all my bones are out of joint.*

Then his smothering brain
began to write to his wife
and three children, the calligraphy
faltering somewhat

> *sorry      for leaving      I miss you so*

> *sorry    we can't hold hands*

> *be faithful my children      be good    pray for me*

> *patawarin mo ako      forgive me      Rosario*

Rosario – her name a prayer.
He could see her so clearly,
hear her voice
in the darkness
as it had sounded
all those nights
of pillow talk, worrying
about the children's scrapes,
chuckling over
a runaway chicken,
making love in whispers
in the stifling heat.

That stupid chicken
almost made him recant.
To be above ground again,
laughing with his family
chasing a bird
back to safety,
breathing the air
of Binondo at dusk – for that,
he almost gave the signal.

His brain signing papers,
stepping on his Savior's face.
His blood, ink.

But he held his hand still.

The miracle of air
never came.
                              Ite, missa est.

His writer's hand
at last unmoving,
his body burned
                    Deo gratias
like paper.
A broken lantern. Smoke.
Ashes in the sea.
                    Alleluia.

# Author's Note

The baybayin phrases in this collection were produced with Tagalog Stylized Baybayin Font created by Paul Morrow (paulmorrow.ca/bayeng1.htm) and used here by permission, with transliteration by the author. The font is a modern composite of many past examples of baybayin characters. It was designed for use on computers and should not be considered an exact replica of historic scripts.

The phrase "Ang hindi marunong lumingon sa pinanggalingan hindi makararating sa paroroonan" is a Filipino proverb sometimes misattributed to Filipino writer and political martyr José Rizal, perhaps due to this line from his play *El consejo de los dioses*: "Con el recuerdo del pasado, entro en el porvenir" (With memory of the past I enter the future).

The word batidor in "Pantoum for a Childhood Elsewhere" refers to a wooden implement used as a whisk for aerating hot chocolate. It comes from the Spanish word for mixer or beater, batidora, and is retained in masculine form in Filipino. Depending on region or family tradition, a derivative word, batirol, or the word used by Spanish colonists in Mexico, molinillo, has also been used for this implement in the Philippines.

ISABEL CRISTINA LEGARDA was born in the Philippines and spent her early childhood there before moving to Bethesda, Maryland. She holds degrees in literature and bioethics and is currently a practicing physician in Boston, Massachusetts. She enjoys writing about women's lived experience, cultural issues, and finding grace in a challenging world. Her work has appeared in *America Magazine, Cleaver, The Dewdrop, The Lowestoft Chronicle, Ruminate, Sky Island Review, Smartish Pace, Qu, West Trestle Review,* and others.

Find Isabel on Instagram and Twitter @poetintheOR.

Thank you for supporting independent publishing.

Yellow Arrow Publishing is a nonprofit supporting
writers and artists identifying as women. Visit
YellowArrowPublishing.com for information on our
publications, workshops, and writing opportunities.

www.ingramcontent.com/pod-product-compliance
Lightning Source LLC
Chambersburg PA
CBHW030502130626
46549CB00007B/2832